THE ULTIMATE TRADING RISK MANAGEMENT GUIDE

STEVE BURNS
HOLLY BURNS

© Copyright 2019, Stolly Media, LLC.

All rights reserved. No part of this publication may be reproduced, distributed, or transmitted in any form or by any means, without the prior written permission of the publisher, except in the case of brief quotations embodied in critical reviews and certain other noncommercial uses permitted by copyright law.

DISCLAIMER

This book is meant to be informational and shouldn't be used as trading or investing advice. All readers should gather information from multiple sources to create their personalized investment strategies and trading systems. The authors make no guarantees related to the claims contained herein. Always seek the advice of a competent licensed professional before implementing any plan or system that involves your money. Please invest and trade responsibly.

INTRODUCTION

"Where you want to be is always in control, never wishing, always trading, and always first and foremost protecting your ass. That's why most people lose money as individual investors or traders because they're not focusing on losing money. They need to focus on the money that they have at risk and how much capital is at risk in any single investment they have. If everyone spent 90 percent of their time on that, not 90 percent of the time on pie-in-the-sky ideas on how much money they're going to make, then they will be incredibly successful investors." – Paul Tudor Jones

---

There is no shortage of entry signals, stock picks, and trading psychology tips, but where are all the risk management books? If you study trading legends you know that risk management is mentioned frequently. This may come as a surprise to people that think billionaire traders are successful and because of their accuracy, assuming that they rarely make mistakes. A significant portion of any successful trader's success is carefully managing risk to avoid losing streaks that destroy their capital, or a large loss that blows up their account.

Risk management is often overlooked and frequently underrated, and yet it's one of the most important aspects of profitable trading. A trader must develop a system with an edge and have the discipline to trade it consistently with the correct position sizing to be successful. Without correct risk management, no trading system will be successful over long periods, because the first large losing streak with improper position sizing will likely be the last.

The goal of this book is to lay out the key principles of risk management, so you can become proficient at keeping your money safe when trading. Keeping your money safe and maintaining positive trading psychology will increase your odds of profitability so you can actively trade long enough to achieve success.

Steve Burns
Follow Me on Twitter and Instagram
New Trader U Blog
New Trader University Courses

1

TRADING & INVESTING RISKS

"Throughout my financial career, I have continually witnessed examples of other people that I have known being ruined by a failure to respect risk. If you don't take a hard look at risk, it will take you." – Larry Hite

Traders and investors are drawn to the financial markets because it provides an opportunity to make money. The profit capabilities are uncapped and the barrier to entry is low. Trading is an equal opportunity endeavor and almost anyone can open a brokerage account for a small amount of money. Someone can open an account in the morning and be trading against professionals that afternoon. Your risk aversion will determine if this sounds exciting or like a terrible idea.

Just because you *can* buy and a semi-tractor trailer and drive it down the Interstate, doesn't mean it wouldn't be incredibly dangerous for you and others. In fact, the barrier to entry on the truck is higher than a trading account. A broker will gladly throw you the keys to your own trading account if you deposit a small sum of money, pay him a low commission fee, and sign a commission agreement. He gets paid when you enter and exit a trade, so he makes money whether you are successful or not. You take on all the risk and they get paid regardless. So, what are the risks?

The trading world is full of pictures of exotic cars and fancy homes depicting success, but you almost never hear about the risks of losing money. The fastest way to lose money is to try and get rich quick. You can lose your trading account with one bad trade if you don't understand leverage or risk exposure. And selling option contracts short with no hedge can cost you more money than you have in your account!

The options and futures markets can be dangerous if you aren't properly capitalized or don't understand the leverage these products can provide; they can be all or nothing bets whether you know it or not. Penny stocks that are sold over the counter (OTC) and on the *pink sheets* can be more risk than they're worth, because many aren't real companies or just pump and dump schemes. Also, the bigger you trade the more liquidity issues you can experience. You can find yourself trapped and unable to get out of a trade or experience large amounts of slippage on exit and entries that cause substantial losses.

There is a big difference between trading with your retirement account savings, trading in a speculative account, and risking capital on all our nothing bets. A retirement account like an IRA, 401k, or 403B should be safeguarded against large risks. Stock indexes are a good long-term vehicle to maintain capital and grow it incrementally year over year with minimal risk. A speculative trading account can be traded more aggressively with individual stocks to try and beat the market, but the best way to grow your trading account is to let it grow over time, slowly compounding your capital.

Risk capital is what traders use for all or nothing bets. You can lose it all, but it won't have a significant impact on your lifestyle or long-term finances. Risk capital is a good designation for most of the trading that goes on with options, futures, forex, penny stock, and crypto-currencies for amateur retail traders. Most trading done by undercapitalized traders in these markets are all or nothing bets, whether they realize it or not. Most options will go in-the-money or expire worthless. Most crypto currencies in 2017-2018 won't be accepted for monetary exchange or go to $0 quickly. Most penny stocks are already under a penny, so they have a shorter trip to zero or becoming too illiquid to exit.

It's crucial to understand the difference in the type of capital you're putting at risk. Do you want to retire with the money? Then it's necessary to be careful and grow it slowly because you have plenty of time. Do you want to grow your trading capital into a large account? Don't spend it, leave your profits in and let them grow. Do you have extra money you want to risk on the hopes of a big win? Be careful, there is a fine line between a trader and a gambler. Even if you're doing it for entertainment and understand that you could lose it all, make sure you don't get caught up in an emotional roller coaster of big wins and big losses.

There are two sides to every coin. If you flip a coin over and over, you will get a mixture of results, sometimes heads and sometimes tails. You wouldn't expect heads or tails every time just based on the odds. Trading is the same way, sometimes you'll make money and sometimes you'll lose money. There isn't a 100% winning system, and the first step on the path of trading success is to realize this fact and stop looking for a perfect system that never loses. Instead, focus on a profitable system that you can let play out over a large sample size of many entries and exits. You must understand that you'll have an equity curve that won't always be making new all-time highs, but there will be a path to profitability and managing losses and losing streaks can be the difference between success or failure.

There is offense and defense in sports; you can both score points and have points scored against you. Investing and trading in the markets is no different. Many people only see the reward and ignore the risk. Yes, you must have winning trades and make money, but you also have to minimize your risk of loss and the size of your losing trades when you have them. Small winning trades don't do you any good if you have big losing trades. Risk management may be more important than stock picks, winning trades, or making money. What is the point of making money if you don't keep it long term?

There are times when risk management is far more important than profits, and keeping the capital you have safe is more important than growing it. Bear markets, crashes, and high volatility environments lead to increased risks and uncertainty, with many traders seeing profits quickly evaporate. Aggressive trading makes money, but defensive risk management keeps it.

It's not only about finding trades to enter, it's also about protecting your account from destruction during high risk environments and large losses. Patterns and trends in a market environment can give you levels of price action to define your risk, like support and resistance lines for example.

The biggest mistake you can make in risk management is finding yourself on the wrong side of a trend with a large position size, stubbornly letting it continue to run against you without exiting. If you don't know what to do in a market the safest thing to do is to go to cash. Your trading plan should have contingencies for volatility and market changes so you can preplan position sizing and the total capital open to risk.

There are many types of risks that a trader must deal with in the financial markets. Here are some of the many risks that a you should be aware of before you place your first trade.

- You have the basic risk that your trade will be a loser, but you can typically control the maximum amount you lose through position size based on volatility and a stop loss at a price level that shows you were wrong.
- You also have the general market risk factor. You can pick a stock of a great company, but if the trend of the stock market itself is down, the likelihood is that your stock will also fall, regardless of the fundamental merits of the

company or the past strength of your stock's price movement. The market is like a tide that comes in and lifts all ships and then goes out and lowers them back down, regardless of the quality of any single boat. Always understand the overall trend of the market you are trading.

- You have the risk of your trading vehicle either being or becoming highly volatile. Volatility risk can spook you into exiting your position too soon or cause your system to stop working because the position you entered hit your predetermined stop loss and forced you to sell. Keep in mind that it could reverse and be back where it started later that same day. Most trading systems are just a process designed to capture a trend by filtering out the volatility with quantified signals for entries and exits.
- Overnight risk is when something unexpected happens when the market is closed, making your trade gap down the next day so you don't have a chance to sell and stop your loss. This risk applies to everyone except day traders or traders who trade markets that are open 24 hours on most days.
- Liquidity risk is when there aren't many buyers or sellers for your trading vehicle, so you lose money in the bid/ask spread. The *bid* is what a market maker is willing to buy your asset for, and the *ask* is what they are offering to sell it for. There are penny stocks and options with low enough volume that you can lose over 10% on your position by buying and selling, even if the quoted price doesn't move. If your buy a trade with an ASK $10.00 and sell it for the BID $9.50, you lose 5% on your capital in the position when you enter and when you exit, for a total loss of 10% due to slippage on the round-trip trade. It's important to trade in stocks and options that have a small spread in the bid/ask quotes,

and remember that there should only be pennies separating them.
- Margin risk is when you use your stocks as collateral and borrow money from your broker to buy additional stocks. After you have set up a margin account, most brokers will allow you to buy additional stocks and double the size of your account holdings. You can use a $10,000 account to buy $20,000 worth of stock if the stocks are marginable securities. Some risky penny stocks, leveraged ETFs, and small cap stocks are not marginable. The good thing about margin is that you make twice as much profit when you're right, but the risk is that you can lose twice as much if you're wrong. Doubling your risk with margin increases your risk of ruin by making your losses compound twice as fast.
- If you're holding a stock through earnings, you're exposed to the risk of a sharp move in one direction after the announcement. It can damage your account if the move is too fast and blows through your stop loss after hours. Earnings can be profitable, but they can also be risky. Earnings can be random in nature, reversing an established trend regardless of how good or bad the earnings report is. News is frequently baked into the price, so trading the trend leading into earnings and after earnings is usually a safer trade than playing the event itself. You will typically have better results if you sell before earnings.
- If you are invested in a company located in a different country or your stock's company does most of its business in a country that suddenly has a change in political power, you could experience political risk. Investors and property owners were wiped out when the Communists seized all private property for the state in Cuba in 1960. Another example on a smaller scale is when Venezuela

seized several oil projects from the American oil company ConocoPhillips in 2007. Unfortunately, there are many more examples of this in history.
- Human error can also play a factor, as there is always the risk of putting one too many zeroes on the number of shares you want to buy, entering the wrong symbol, or selling a stock short instead of buying it long. Double checking your trades before you place them is critical to your success.
- Technology risk can be frustrating. As if trading isn't hard enough, you run the risk of your Internet connection crashing or your broker's trading platform going down in the middle of a trade. It's a good idea to have multiple devices for executing trades. Different types of internet connections like a smart phone connection to back up your Wi-Fi, as well as the pre-programmed phone number for your broker so you can contact them instantly. Anything can happen while you're trading so always have a Plan B.

2

RISK/REWARD RATIOS

> *"1:5 risk /reward means I'm risking one dollar to make five. What five to one does is allow you to have a hit ratio of 20%. I can actually be a complete imbecile. I can be wrong 80% of the time, and I'm still not going to lose."* – Paul Tudor Jones

We expose our capital to risk whenever we enter a trade. Our returns come from the positions we take and the magnitude of risk we take on in pursuit of profits. Risk and reward are two sides of the same coin; the risk of the loss creates the potential for the gain. The quest for the *Holy Grail* trading system is an attempt to eliminate risk and never lose. If a trading system never lost, you would quickly own the world through compounding gains. There's no way to remove the risk from the reward, but a key principle of profitable trading, investing, and speculation is to know when to take on risk for maximum profitability. You should only take trades where the profit opportunity outweighs the risk. The risk must be worth the reward.

As traders chase hot stocks, trends, and chart patterns, they frequently forget the importance of taking trades that have the potential for large wins or small losses. Big losses will kill your account quickly and small wins will do little to pay for those losses. Trades must be asymmetric; the downside risk is carefully planned and managed, but the upside profits are open-ended. This is a critical part of trading success.

The risk/reward ratio is used by more experienced traders to compare the expected profits of a trade to the amount of money risked capturing profits. This ratio is calculated mathematically by dividing the amount of profit the trader expects when the position is closed (the reward) by the amount the trader could lose if price moves in the unprofitable direction and the trader is stopped out for a loss (the risk).

The following chart illustrates that in order to remain profitable, the bigger your wins are versus your losses, the lower your winning percentage must be.

Risk	Reward	Breakeven Win Rate %
50	1	98%
10	1	91%
5	1	83%
3	1	75%
2	1	67%
1	1	50%
1	2	33%
1	3	25%
1	5	17%
1	10	9%
1	50	2%

Risk/Reward Ratio needed for a win rate to break even

Most profitable traders understand that the winning percentage for the best traders is only about 50%-60% regardless of trading or investing method. Having big winning trades and small losing trades is a trading edge. Large losses are the primary cause of unprofitable trading across all time frames and methods.

The skill of cutting losses short is a primary driver of a profitable trader's ability to make money. Big losses cause large drawdowns in capital and skew the risk/reward ratio against the trader making profitability mathematically difficult. One large loss can wipe out a significant amount of small winning trades. Small losses are necessary in order to maintain a profitable risk/reward ratio, and loss size determines the winning percent needed for profitability.

- With a 1:1 risk/reward ratio and 50%-win rate, a trader breaks even.*
- With a 2:1 risk/reward ratio and about a 35%-win rate, a trader breaks even.*
- With a 3:1 risk/reward ratio and about a 25%-win rate, a trader breaks even.*

Excluding commissions and slippage.

The larger your winning trades are versus your losing trades, the lower your win rate must be to become profitable. The lower your win rate must be, the better your odds are that you'll be profitable as a trader. You don't have to be right all the time, you just need to be right big and wrong small.

To determine your risk/reward ratio, determine where price must go to show that your expected outcome is likely incorrect. This is the key price support level and where you'll need to place your stop loss. You can set your profit target for a rally to a key resistance level or a new all-time high, and that will be your potential profit target. Your stop loss level is your risk if your trade is wrong, and your target areas are your rewards if you're right. Allowing one of the two to play out is the key to skewing your risk/reward ratio in your favor and increasing your odds of profitability.

Letting a loser run through your stop loss to create a large loss or taking a profit too quickly and eliminating a big winning trade can undermine the risk/reward ratio and create unprofitable trading conditions. High winning percentages are difficult for most traders, especially with tight stop losses. It's simpler and more profitable to ride trends in your trading time frame.

A great formula to use is a 3:1 risk/reward ratio. Let's use this formula to see what happens if a trader risks $100 to make $300. If 100 shares of stock are bought for $30 a share and the stop is at $29, then the stock should only be purchased if it's probable that the stock could run to $33. Profits could be taken at $33 a share, but if it runs to $34, a trailing stop could be set at $33 to give the stock an opportunity to be a bigger winner. Remember to set the trailing stop to lock in the $3 per share gain.

Following this plan, your account could look like this after ten trades.

- Lose $100
- Make $300
- Lose $100
- Make $300
- Lose $100
- Make $300
- Lose $100
- Make $300
- Lose $100
- Make $300

Profit is $1,000 with only a 50%-win rate.

However, if you allow losers to run, hoping they will come back so you can take profits on a rebound, then you can get into trouble fast.

What if the stock you were trading fell from $30 to $29, you didn't stop out, and it kept falling to $20? What if you wanted to lock in profits at $31 and not let your winner run? The dynamics of your risk/reward ratio would change, leaving you unprofitable even though you had an 80%-win rate.

- Lose $1000
- Make $100
- Lose $500
- Make $200
- Make $100
- Make $100
- Make $200
- Make $100
- Make $100
- Make $100

Loss is $500 even with an 80%-win rate.

Remember that you can cut losses short if you are proven wrong before your stop is hit, but at the same time you must allow enough room for normal fluctuations and volatility, and use position sizing that you're comfortable with for your trading account size. The above examples kept it simple so the math would be easy to understand. You must take each stock's volatility into account along with your own time frame for stop placement. Every trading vehicle will have different dynamics of price action. Individual stop losses must be placed carefully based on the chart pattern. Set it at the location where price shouldn't go below if your trade is right.

- Allow winners to run as far as possible with the use of trailing stops; you could have a huge win with the right entry and trend.
- Know how much you will risk on any one trade, and don't enter a trade where the upside is not at least three times your risk of loss if your stop is hit.

Stop losses are tools for minimizing losses so you stop a small loss from becoming a big loss. A profit target based on technical price levels or indicators lets you quantify whether the reward is good enough to take the risk. A trailing stop loss is a tool for maximizing your reward by both locking in profits while they are there, and letting a winning trade run as far as it will go, only exiting at the end of a trend when it stops going higher.

It's not the winning percentage of a trader that determines their profitability, but the size of all their winning trades versus the size of all their losing trades. This is the math that determines profitability.

3

WHEN TO STOP YOUR LOSS

"Whenever I enter a position, I have a predetermined stop. That's the only way I can sleep at night. I know where I'm getting out before I get in." – Bruce Kovner

Traders are unprofitable because their losses knock out all their previous gains. There are many remedies for big losses. Position sizing properly will limit the size of a loss when wrong. A stop loss is an early signal to get out of a trade when it looks like it is going to be a loser. A psychological dynamic often comes into play and emotions take over. Ego doesn't want to take a stop a loss because it wants to hold it and hope it comes back. Traders often don't want to admit a trade is a loser, because then they feel like a loser.

The aversion to loss makes traders let losers run because they think the results aren't final until they close the trade. Traders must learn to cut a loser short because losses can cause a system to be unprofitable regardless of other dynamics. Too much open risk and leverage with no plan to stop a loss can cause any trader to lose their account. A stop loss is your first line of defense in risk management.

A stop loss sets the predetermined risk for your trade in monetary terms. You know at what price level you're getting out when you get in. A stop loss is the quantified price risk level that will tell you that you're wrong if the trade goes that far against you.

If you went back and removed your biggest losses over the past few months or years, what would your trading results look like? Many successful traders, including myself, have done this and it can be enlightening. The major factors that can make you unprofitable or cause big drawdowns in capital are the big losses. The root of a large loss is usually the result of emotion and ego and not a market event.

A large loss is almost always caused by being on the wrong side of a trend and then staying there. That's why it's so important to have a trading plan before you enter a trade, so you know where you'll exit if you're wrong. A plan allows you to formulate your strategy with clarity and decide what to do based on the math *before* you're in a losing situation. This eliminates having to make decisions when emotions are running high. Here are a few of the root causes for big losses and what you can do about them.

- Too stubborn to exit when proven wrong: You refuse to take a loss and think a loss isn't real if you don't exit the trade and lock in the paper losses. You set your own stop loss based on your own strategy, time frame, and goals. It's critical that you respect your own exit plan for losses. A failure to respect your own plan can lead to a loss in faith in your own discipline. It's necessary that you believe in your ability to trade.
- Too much ego to take a loss: You are on the wrong side of the market trend but think if you hold a losing position you can be proven right on a reversal. While you are waiting to be proven right your loss gets bigger and bigger. Ironically, nothing can damage a trader's ego more

than big losses. Admitting a trade isn't going to work out isn't personal, it's just math. The more mechanical and systematic you can make your trading, the less your ego will be engaged and the more profitable you will become.
- Too much hope for a reversal: You think the market can't keep moving against you and must reverse at current price levels. Uptrends have no long-term resistance and downtrends have no long-term support. Trends can become parabolic and move farther than anyone believed possible. Sometimes, price doesn't revert to the mean, and trends can stay irrational and keep going against you. Exiting a losing trade at your stop loss saves the mental and emotional stress of experiencing a growing loss for hours and days. Just get out, you can always get back in.
- Trading too big a position size: The bigger you trade the bigger your potential loss and the more likely that your emotions will override your trading plan. Don't trade a big enough position size that it becomes difficult for you to take a stop loss emotionally. Trade with a size that keeps your mind in control of your trading execution.
- Buying in a downtrend: Staying bullish in bear markets loses money as markets make lower highs and lower lows. All stocks will eventually roll over in a bear market, no matter how great the underlying business or fundamentals. You can love a company or business model, but the chart must agree with your opinion.
- Selling short in an uptrend: Staying bearish in a bull market will lose money as the market makes higher highs and higher lows. Always stay positioned in the direction of least resistance in open trades.
- No trading plan: When you don't have a plan for your trades you are planning to fail. When you don't have an exit plan or entry strategy you can get confused when faced with losses on a trade you thought was a sure thing.

It can be paralyzing when faced with a loss that was unexpected. Written plans are meant to be a solution to the emotional dilemmas created by unexpected events. You look to your trading plan for a good option instead of making a bad emotional decision in the heat of the moment.
- No trading system: If you don't have a quantified and proven price action trading system then your trades are just guesses. Large losses can happen due to the random nature of trading with no plan or system. If your entries and exits are based on opinions, predictions, and feelings instead of a quantified backtest, you're headed for disaster.
- Bad position sizing parameters: Big losses will occur when position sizing is not based on historical volatility and worst-case scenarios. Without using math for position sizing, you run the risk of hubris and ego convincing you to trade beyond your means.
- No discipline: If you don't have the time or patience to create a systematic trading process and the discipline to follow a predetermined method, you are unlikely to be successful. Taking your stop loss at the level you planned requires discipline, self-control, and acceptance of the loss.

To figure out your stop loss level ask yourself, "What is the specific price level this trade can go to before it proves that I was wrong and I need to exit?" A stop loss should be given enough room so you aren't shaken out prematurely with normal price action, but it should be placed at a level that signals that something has changed from your initial entry and you are likely wrong about the trade. Here are some ways to quantify a stop loss on a trade at entry.

- One of the most popular stop losses is at a level of long-

term price support for a long position, or a price level of resistance for a short trade. Swing traders place their stop losses at this level because they think a breakout of a range changes the market from range-bound to trending, and the trade may continue to trend against them.
- Moving averages are another place that stop losses are placed. The moving average would depend on the time frame of the trade. Single moving average filters should be meaningful for the time frame used and account for the volatility of the current price action.
- Moving average crossovers are another option for a systematic place to exit a loss. There are mechanical trading systems where you enter a trend trade when a shorter moving average crosses over a longer one and then exit when the shorter term moving average crosses back under the longer one. This provides a volatility filter for price action with fewer false signals than a single moving average.
- Use a time stop: Set a time limit on how long you will allow a trade to move a certain amount. If it fails to move far enough and fast enough, you can get out. If you're not making money, you're exposing yourself to risk without an upside. Don't stay in flat trades, rather use your money to make money with better opportunities.
- Volatility stop: Stop out if the market or your stock has a large expansion in its daily price range or starts moving against you. Either decrease your position size or get out of the trade due to increased risk based on volatility expansion. The ATR (Average True Range) is one way to quantify this.
- Sell your position because you have found a better trade with a greater probability of success. Depending on your available capital, there are times you can exit a losing trade for a better opportunity, even if your stop loss hasn't

been hit. Also, your risk/reward dynamic may have diminished in your current trade and you may find better profit potential in another trade.
- Stop losses can be taken instantly intra-day, end of day, the next morning, end of week, or end of the month. This depends on the time frame you're trading on.
- Stop losses can be automated with your broker or taken manually.
- A trailing stop is not the same as a stop loss. A stop loss is the way you exit a losing trade to avoid a large loss. A trailing stop is how you exit a winning trade by raising your stop behind your winning trade as it trends in your favor. When price action reverses and hits that trailing stop, you sell. A trailing stop can be a short-term moving average or a percentage of your open profit. A trailing stop is how you lock in profits on a winning trade as the momentum slows and then reverses.

If you want to be a profitable trader, you must learn to manage stop losses. This is not optional. A stop losses' job is to keep losses small, but it must be set in a place that allows enough room for a winning trade to play out without getting stopped out prematurely.

4

TRAILING STOP LOSSES

"I set protective stops at the same time I enter a trade. I normally move those stops in to lock in a profit as the trend continues." – Ed Seykota

Trailing stop losses are tools for managing open profits as a winning trade evolves and the distance between current price and the original stop loss expands. A trailing stop is defined as moving your stop loss from the original location at entry to a new price that is closer to the current price level. A trailing stop loss is triggered the same way as a stop loss, by price reversing back through that stop level.

Using a trailing stop loss is a good way to protect open profits in capital on a trading position. Open profits on a winning trade are only paper profits until the trade is exited to lock in profits. Celebrating a winning trade before it closes is premature at best and dangerous at worst. A trailing stop loss is a plan for minimizing loss if the trade does start to reverse against you, and a way to let your winning trade run if the trend continues.

You can use short term moving averages, moving average crossovers, an Average True Range (ATR) retracement, a close below the previous day's low, volatility expansion, or a candlestick reversal pattern as technical indicators for placing trailing stops. The goal of trailing stops, like stop losses, is to put the trailing stop loss at a level that shouldn't be reached if the trend is going to continue.

Trailing stops can help filter the noise in price action and establish a better emotional balance. Because all your open profits are not at risk and you have capped the loss to a set level, it should reduce the stress of letting a winner run. Risking open profits gives traders the opportunity to capture larger profits in a trend. Trailing stops are the best of both worlds; defensive for the current profits but open-ended for the profit growth.

Traders should take defensive measures to protect their open profits before they worry about making money in a market trend. As a trade progresses in a trader's favor, the risk/reward ratio shifts against the original entry and stop loss placement. The same reward isn't constant as a trend emerges. A trailing stop is a way to detect when a trend is bending and the probability of a greater return on a winning trade is decreasing. You don't want to profit and then see it evaporate, taking you back to even or worse. A trailing stop loss is a dynamic way to manage an open trade and the risk/reward ratio based on price action rather than opinions, emotions, or predictions. A profit target is a fixed way to manage an open trade because it can cap and limit the upside. A trailing stop leaves the profit potential open and only risks part of the open profits at risk in order to let the winner run.

Using trailing stops allows you to capture most of a trend and only exit when the trend starts to bend. Using a structured trailing stop loss helps to limit emotional trading by letting price action influence the plan of action. All trader should wait and execute the plan for the trailing the stop in their time frame, and if the trend continues, move the trailing stop to the next logical price level. By using trailing stops, trading accounts are protected from unpleasant volatility that can take back open profits.

One downside of trailing stops that they can give back some open profits in the pursuit of more profits. They don't allow you to exit at peak profits, instead they wait and see what happens next. This isn't anything to worry about, because most people can't perfectly time the most profitable entry and exit. The best opportunity for profit is to catch as much of a trend as possible, wait for a trend signal to emerge, and then ride the trend until the end when it bends.

Trailing stops are a great money management tool because they help you decide how much open profits you are willing to risk in the pursuit of more profits. Using trailing stops helps you exit a winning trade when the reward stops being worth the risk and move on to better trading opportunities with better setups.

A trailing stop loss is a risk management tool to limit the return of open profits in a winning trade, while maximizing potential profits big wins with better risk/reward ratios.

This is an example of a recent trend trade using trailing stops.

1. I entered $AGQ at $23.25 at the end of the day on 12/6/18 based on the 5-day / 20-day EMA crossover. My initial profit target was the 70 RSI and the 200-day SMA.
2. I set the 5-day EMA/20-day EMA cross under as the initial stop loss signal on entry.
3. I set the close below the 20-day EMA as the initial trailing stop loss signal as it started to be profitable
4. When the trend got under way, I moved my trailing stop loss to the 5-day EMA.
5. As price accelerated beyond the 5-day EMA, I moved the trailing stop loss to a close under the previous day's price low.
6. As $AGQ broke the 200-day SMA and the 70 RSI, I

moved my trailing stop to a close back under the 200-day SMA or the 70 RSI. I would lock in profits based on either of those closes.

7. I exited $AGQ at $27.03 for a +16.26% gain on capital at risk because price looked like it was not going to close over the 200-day SMA on 1/4/2019.

Chart Courtesy of StockCharts.com

5

A GUIDE TO POSITION SIZING

"Here's the essence of risk management: Risk no more than you can afford to lose, and also risk enough so that a win is meaningful. If there is no such amount, don't play." – Ed Seykota

Many people want to manage their own trading and investment portfolios, but few consider the importance of disciplined and quantified position sizing strategies. Historical bear markets have shown traders and investors the risk involved in large position sizes without an exit strategy. Proper position sizing is a pillar of successful trading. It's critical that correct position sizing parameters are used to determine how many shares or contracts to trade at an entry signal.

Position sizing and risk exposure show whether you have enough capital to trade additional positions to your current holdings, while stop losses show you where the price must go for you to exit your position. The position sizing aspect of your risk management will determine how much you lose if your stop loss is triggered and you exit your trade for a loss.

Trading must start with the correct position sizing to manage your risk exposure. Once you understand your position sizing inside a quantified trading system, your ability to execute it with discipline will determine your success. If you don't manage your risk through proper position sizing, you will eventually be ruined regardless of any other factors.

Position sizing optimizes capital usage. Few can view all their positions in context of the net risk exposure. Position sizing formulas are crucial for keeping past profits while limiting the future risk of big losses.

Here are some questions you should answer about your own position sizing.

- How much capital will you place on each trade? What percent of total trading capital will you risk on one position?
- What will be the maximum portfolio *heat* on your trading? How much can your account go down in one day if all your positions go against you to the maximum stop loss? How much total risk exposure do you have?
- Do you trade the same during a losing streak? Do you decrease your trade size during losing streaks?
- How do you prepare if trading both long and short positions? What will your position sizing be for the long or short side? Will they be the same?
- Does a portfolio of long and short positions allow you to trade more positions? How do they correlate for total risk exposure?
- How will you adjust for accumulated new profits? Do you trade bigger positions as your account grows? Will you have a system for withdrawing profits, or will you

leave your profits in your account and compound your gains?
- How is volatility handled? What filters for volatility will you use to adjust your position size and stop losses?
- Have you backtested your positions sizing? What size drawdown do you expect during a losing streak based on your win percentage and potential losing streak?

Position sizing is a crucial part of risk management because it can determine the success of a long-term trading system. The size of your trade can also affect your ability to follow your trading system and prevent large losses because you limit your emotional influence on the process.

Position sizing is determined by the placement of your technical stop loss. The stop loss comes first, then your position size is based on the loss you would take if your stop loss is triggered and you exit the trade for a loss. I base position sizing on the principal that I never want to lose more than 1% of my total trading capital on any one trade.

If I am trading with a $100,000 account, I don't want to lose more than $1,000 on a losing trade. A stop loss level must start at the price level that you know you are wrong, and work back to position sizing. If the support level on your trade is $105 for your entry and you set your stop at $100, then you can trade 200 shares with a stop at the $100 price level. 200 X $105 = $21,000 position size for 200 shares. This is about 20% of your total trading capital with around a 5% stop loss on your positions, equaling a 1% loss of your total trading capital.

- A 20% position size of your total trading capital gives you a 5% stop loss on your position to equal 1% of total trading capital.
- A 10% position size of your total trading capital gives you

a 10% stop loss on your position to equal 1% of total trading capital.
- A 5% position size of your total trading capital gives you a 20% stop loss on your position to equal 1% of total trading capital.

The average true range (ATR) can give you the daily range of price movement and help you position size based on your time frame and stock volatility. If your entry is $105, your stop is $100, and the ATR is $1, then you have five days' worth of movement against you as a stop.

Start with your stop loss level and volatility to get your position size. The more room you have on your stop determines how large your position size can be.

If you only risk losing 1% of your trading capital when you are wrong, every trade can become just one of the next 100 with little emotional impact. This principle can help you survive losing streaks and increase your odds of success.

Your position size determines the magnitude of the risk you are willing to expose yourself to for a reward. Different markets can have different types of position sizing.

A good position sizing parameter I have used for a portfolio of individual stocks has been 10% capital for each stock. I try to not have more than six that are too closely correlated. Six technology growth stocks for a 60% total capital allocation would be my maximum position sizing. I would carry more positions if they were less similar, like a utility, consumer staples stock, Real Estate ETF (Exchange Traded Fund), Precious metal ETF, or commodity ETF.

For example, if my entry signals were triggered, then my maximum risk would be positions like this:

- $AMZN 10% of total trading capital.
- $ETSY 10% of total trading capital.
- $FB 10% of total trading capital.

- $TWTR 10% of total trading capital.
- $SQ 10% of total trading capital.
- $PYPL 10% of total trading capital.
- 40% of capital would be in cash or other non-correlated positions.

However, if you are diversified across sectors of the stock market when a correction or bear market comes along, all sectors, stocks, and indexes can move more in sync to the downside as equities as an asset class come under distribution. A strong bear market and downtrend will eventually bring everything down, because fund managers must liquidate their positions to cover withdrawals from their funds.

One benefit of trading a portfolio of stocks position sized conservatively is that a single stock won't do much damage. A 10% drop in any one stock would only be a 1% loss to your total trading capital. Even a 20% plunge in one stock would only be a 2% loss in your account. Proper position sizing based on volatility and your stop loss placement is how you keep your losses in check.

Position sizing is different with option contracts because they can be all or nothing bets, especially with shorter term weekly and front month options. I have successfully used the 1% total capital at risk for my option trades. For example, if I was trading options with a $100,000 account, my maximum option contract position size could be $1,000. Even with an adverse move against the underlining asset that brought my option to zero, my maximum loss would be 1% of my total trading capital.

Option contracts are bets on a specific time frame and price action, they aren't assets and can deteriorate rapidly, with most expiring worthless. A stop loss is difficult to set on an option because they must be set based on technical levels on a chart rather than price moves. The simplest path is to limit the position size on an option contract at open, so the worst-case scenario won't result in a big loss.

Options are asymmetric trading vehicles. The upside with leverage means that they can provide many times greater upside than the capital at risk. Options are designed to give the opportunity for big wins, but it's critical that you position size correctly to avoid the big losses.

Ed Seykota said, "I intend to risk below 5% on a trade, allowing for poor executions." This quote gives us a clue about his own position sizing. Ed was a trend follower with diversified futures contracts. A 5% position size makes sense with futures contracts, because they apply leverage to capital on the commodity, and they give the rights to buy and sell.

Here are my suggested guidelines for position sizing account capital in different markets.

- 25% position sizing for stock index ETFs.
- 10% position sizing for individual stocks.
- 5% for futures contracts.
- 1% for options contracts.
- Manage your position size carefully when you trade.
- Adjust your position sizing based on volatility.
- Know where you will get out before you get in.
- Your preplanned position sizing parameters will determine the number of contracts or shares you trade in all markets.

6

THE 1% LOSS PER TRADE RULE

"The very first rule we live by is: Never risk more than 1% of total equity on any trade." – Larry Hite

"I try very hard not to risk more than 1% of my portfolio on a single trade." – Bruce Kovnar

One of the most important rules a trader can learn is never risk more than 1% of your trading account on a single trade. This doesn't mean trading with 1% of your account capital, it means adjusting your stops and position sizes based on the volatility of your stock, currency, commodity, option, or futures contract.

This rule helps you avoid large drawdowns because when you're wrong, it's just 1% of your total trading capital. Not only does this rule eliminate your risk of ruin on a string of losing trades or on one big one, but it also lowers your stress level so you can trade with a clear head.

Going back to our $100,000 trading account example, let's look at combining your stop loss level with your position size. In this account, if you buy $10,000 worth of a stock as a position size with a stock price of $100, you set your stop loss for a drop to a $90 stock price. When you are stopped out, your new position size is $9,000, and when you exit at $90, you have lost $1,000 (1%) of your total trading capital leaving you with $99,000.

If you haven't had a string of losing trades in a row, you haven't been trading long enough to experience a volatile market or an unexpected event that shakes a stock, commodity, currency or an entire market. The 1% rule gives the trader a maximum level of loss they should suffer when they structure their position sizing in correlation with their stop loss.

If you have six open trades and all of them hit your stop loss at the same time on the same day, you should only experience a drawdown of 6% on your capital. This trade management structure also helps manage your portfolio heat when everything goes against you.

Another benefit to this risk management strategy is that it lets your winners run. With your stop loss safe, you can keep profiting from a trend until it reverses. This is the offensive side of the rule. While your losses shouldn't be more than 1% of trading capital, your wins can be 2%, 3%, 5% or more. Remember that a 1% loss to your total trading capital is the *maximum* loss, you don't have to lose 1% every time you're wrong, you can always risk less based on your account size.

Let's look at an example of how the 1% rule fits in with the risk/reward ratio. On a $100,000 account, you risk $1,000 to make $2,000, $3,000, or $5,000 or more. If you risk 0.50%, then you are risking $500 to make $1,000, $1,500, $2,500 or more. If volatility permits, you could double your position size to $20,000 on a $100,000 account and set your stop loss at a 5% move on the underlying stock for a better risk/reward ratio. The important thing is to consistently apply the 1% total risk rule.

Your trade entries should be designed at a price level and a position size that, if after you enter a trade and it retraces to your stop loss, it only decreases your trading capital by 1% when you exit for a small loss. Small losses and big wins are the secret to success.

A trader's primary job is not to make money, but to protect what they already have so they can continue to grow their capital over time.

7

THE RISK OF RUIN

"The key to long-term survival and prosperity has a lot to do with the money management techniques incorporated into the technical system." – Ed Seykota

The following examples illustrate outcomes alternating between wins and losses of the same magnitude over ten trades. The first chart shows the destruction of capital based on different percentages of risk per trade of total assets under management, with the first column on this chart displaying the total loss of capital if your trade goes against you. This first chart also shows the severity of destruction in a trading account with the same 50%-win rate and the same percentage of loss or gain for each trade on ten different accounts.

The second image shows the magnitude of a drawdown based on a ten trade losing streak, using ten different risk percentage of an account per trade for 10 different parameters.

10 trades with a 50% win rate											
		Trade #1	Trade #2	Trade #3	Trade #4	Trade #5	Trade #6	Trade #7	Trade #8	Trade #9	Trade #10
AUM risk per trade	Start	Win	Loss	Win	Loss	Win	Loss	Win	Loss	Win	Loss
1%	$100,000	$101,000	$99,990	$100,990	$99,980	$100,980	$99,970	$100,970	$99,960	$100,960	$99,950
2%	$100,000	$102,000	$99,960	$101,959	$99,920	$101,918	$99,880	$101,878	$99,840	$101,837	$99,800
3%	$100,000	$103,000	$99,910	$102,907	$99,820	$102,815	$99,730	$102,722	$99,640	$102,630	$99,551
5%	$100,000	$105,000	$99,750	$104,738	$99,501	$104,476	$99,252	$104,214	$99,004	$103,954	$98,756
10%	$100,000	$110,000	$99,000	$108,900	$98,010	$107,811	$97,030	$106,759	$96,060	$105,656	$95,099
15%	$100,000	$115,000	$97,750	$112,413	$95,551	$109,883	$93,401	$107,411	$91,299	$104,994	$89,245
20%	$100,000	$120,000	$96,000	$115,200	$92,160	$110,592	$88,474	$106,168	$84,935	$101,922	$81,537
30%	$100,000	$130,000	$91,000	$118,300	$82,810	$107,653	$75,357	$97,964	$68,575	$89,147	$62,403
40%	$100,000	$140,000	$84,000	$117,600	$70,560	$98,764	$59,270	$82,979	$49,787	$69,702	$41,821
50%	$100,000	$150,000	$75,000	$112,500	$56,250	$84,375	$42,188	$63,281	$31,641	$47,461	$23,730

10 losses in a row											
AUM risk per trade	Start	Loss	Loss	Loss	Loss	Loss	Loss	Loss	Loss	Loss	% Down After 10 Losses
1%	$100,000	$99,000	$98,010	$97,030	$96,060	$95,099	$94,148	$93,207	$92,274	$91,352	$90,438	-9.56%
2%	$100,000	$98,000	$96,040	$94,119	$92,237	$90,392	$88,584	$86,813	$85,076	$83,375	$81,707	-18.29%
3%	$100,000	$97,000	$94,090	$91,267	$88,529	$85,873	$83,297	$80,798	$78,374	$76,023	$73,742	-26.26%
5%	$100,000	$95,000	$90,250	$85,738	$81,451	$77,378	$73,509	$69,834	$66,342	$63,025	$59,874	-40.13%
10%	$100,000	$90,000	$81,000	$72,900	$65,610	$59,049	$53,144	$47,830	$43,047	$38,742	$34,868	-65.13%
15%	$100,000	$85,000	$72,250	$61,413	$52,201	$44,371	$37,715	$32,058	$27,249	$23,162	$19,687	-80.31%
20%	$100,000	$80,000	$64,000	$51,200	$40,960	$32,768	$26,214	$20,972	$16,777	$13,422	$10,737	-89.26%
30%	$100,000	$70,000	$49,000	$34,300	$24,010	$16,807	$11,765	$8,235	$5,765	$4,035	$2,825	-97.18%
40%	$100,000	$60,000	$36,000	$21,600	$12,960	$7,776	$4,666	$2,799	$1,680	$1,008	$605	-99.40%
50%	$100,000	$50,000	$25,000	$12,500	$6,250	$3,125	$1,563	$781	$391	$195	$98	-99.90%

Risk of Ruin

Your capital can stay relatively intact with a 50%-win rate, even with a 10% risk per trade, but it does start to have issues when you attempt to go to 15% or more. The first example is of a neutral system; a 1:1 risk/reward ratio with a 50%-win rate should give you an even outcome most of the time. The losses in this first example highlight the destruction of a drawdown. When you lose 10%, you only need an 11% gain to get back to even. However, when you lose 20% of your trading capital, you need a 25% return on your capital to get back to even. This escalates as you lose more.

If you lose 50% of your account, you need a 100% return to get back to even. A 50% loss on $100,000 drops your account to $50,000, and a 100% return on $50,000 takes you back to $100,000. If you cut your trading account in half, you must *double* it to get back to where you started. The inverse is also true. If you have a 100% return on a $100,000 account and increase it to $200,000, and then have a 50% drawdown, you're back where you started. Drawdowns cut more to the downside than gains help to the upside, because a drawdown destroys capital so you're working from a smaller amount of money.

Position sizing and loss size as a percentage of your account is important because smaller capital gives you less compounding power. Excessive position sizing and high percentage capital risk is dangerous because equal size wins and equal size losses aren't equal in the end; large losses will eventually destroy capital do to this compounding effect.

The second image shows the effect of ten different loss sizes as a percentage of your trading capital on ten different accounts. Remember, this is the same outcome of a string of ten losses on all accounts. The size of the loss on a percentage basis of the capital is the only difference in these losses. You can see that the size of the risk plays a big part in the outcome. The bigger the drawdown, the higher return you must have to get back to even. One surprising outcome is that the 1% loss account had less than a 10% drawdown, while the 2% loss per trade had less than a 20% drawdown. How is this possible? Because you're using a fixed percentage of risk per trade, you risk less when your account is smaller and more when it grows larger. With a $100,000 account and 1% risk parameter per trade, you're risking a $1,000 per trade. With $99,000 you would risk $990 per trade, and at $90,000 you would only risk $900.

This defensive strategy with a fixed bet size helps slow down your drawdown by decreasing your losses on the way down. The inverse is true because you would increase your risk size during winning streaks as your account grows. At $110,000 you would start risking $1,100 per trade, helping to compound your capital. This principal helps to increase your returns and minimize your drawdowns using proper position sizing parameters.

One of the main reasons that traders fail is because they don't understand the concept of capital destruction. The more capital you risk per trade, the quicker you'll experience a large drawdown during a losing streak. You must overcome not only the financial drawdown, but also the hit to your mental and emotional well-being. It's difficult to maintain your enthusiasm for trading when you consistently lose money. Also, your discipline can be negatively impacted as your desire to speed up the recovery process can lead to more bad decisions and more drawdowns.

No matter how good you are, you can't trade so large that a single losing streak is your last. If you risk too much of your trading capital, even a few losses in a 50%-win rate streak will destroy your capital. You're not going to be perfect as a trader, that's why it's crucial to protect your trading account from big losses and destructive losing streaks that can be difficult to comeback from financially, mentally, and emotionally. You *will* eventually have streaks of 50%-win rates and losing streaks of ten trades in a row regardless of your trading system. The question is, will you survive them with your current risk exposure per trade? To be successful, you must structure your position sizing so your losses don't destroy your capital after every losing streak.

- A 10% loss requires an 11% return to get back to even.
- A loss of 20% of your capital requires a 25% return to get back to even.
- A 50% loss of capital needs a 100% return just to get back to where you started.
- Risking 1% of your capital per trade puts you down 10% after 10 trades.
- Risking 5% per trade puts you down 50% after 10 trades.

8

DANGERS OF CORRELATION & BENEFITS OF DIVERSIFICATION

"If you diversify, control your risk, and go with the trend, it just has to work." – Larry Hite.

Many traders and investors trade in only one asset class, and some only trade one sector or type of stock. The stock market is a popular place for retail traders, and it's the place to be long in a bull market when there are expectations of increased corporate earnings and the economy is growing. You can do well only trading stocks if you follow the trend or stay out of them when price action doesn't favor your signals and system.

Stocks have traditionally risen over ten-year periods, beating most other asset classes in the long term. But it's important to note that just because it's been that way in the past, doesn't mean it will stay that way. And stocks aren't the place to be in 20% bear market corrections, flat price periods, or when the market is volatile.

Success comes from capturing trends inside your trading or investing time frame. The better the entry and the longer the time frame, the better chance you will make money. Stocks don't always trend, but you can usually find trends if you expand your watch list, systems, and backtests.

In addition to equities, there are forex, futures, bonds, and option contract markets. Trend followers increase their odds of catching outsized trends and increasing profits by trading multiple markets. If you only trade one market or one type of system and price action isn't lining up with your signals, you're limiting your possibilities and decreasing your chance of success. Trading markets that are not correlated gives you a wider range of opportunities with different types of price action.

People that trade only stocks have more correlation risk than they realize, especially if they are long only traders. This is great during bull markets, but it can lead to large losses during bear markets. If someone who is employing this strategy is holding ten volatile stocks at the same time and the stock market gaps down, they can be in big trouble. If their stop loss is risking 1% of their capital per stop, and all ten are triggered at the same time, their account is down 10% in one day. If they are risking more of their capital than 1% or have more than ten positions on at one time with the help of leverage or margin, they can lose a substantial amount in a market drawdown. If they are holding six equity positions but also have gold, oil, bonds, or a currency, there is less chance of a significant loss because these assets are not as correlated, and it would be rare for all of them to go against the trader at once. Holding both long and short positions in short selling strategies can help diversify a portfolio and lower correlation risk, because it would be unusual for a short and a long position to go against you at the same time.

The great thing about the modern stock market is there are now Exchange Traded Funds that can help with stock portfolio diversification. The more concentrated a trade is, the more profitable it can be if you're right, but the risk is greater if you're wrong. The more diversified your trading positions are the less accurate you must be to make money. When equities under an asset class are under accumulation, indexes can capture leading stocks. A high yield bond ETF can diversify your risk and having a position in winning stocks can lead to large gains over time.

Let's examine asset classes to see how focused our trades can get. Here's an example of what a diversified watchlist of different asset classes using exchange traded funds might look like.

- $VTI (The Vanguard Total Stock Market ETF)
- $DBC (Commodity Index Tracking Fund)
- $GLD (Gold)
- $SLV (Silver)
- $USO (Oil)
- $AGG (Aggregate Bond ETF)
- $TLT (20 Year Treasury Bonds)
- $IEF (Intermediate Term Bonds)
- $JNK (High Yield Bonds)
- $HYG (High Yield Corporate Bonds)
- $UUP (U.S. Dollar Index Fund)

This list gives ETF options for holding the total US stock market and different asset classes outside of equities, commodities as an asset class or metals and energy, also bonds of different risk levels and duration, and a currency. This gives you the option of rotating to a different asset class if there is a trend.

On the index level we can diversify by market cap.

- $DIA (Mega Cap)
- $SPY (Big Cap)
- $QQQ (NASDAQ Big Cap)
- $IWM (Small Cap)
- $IWC (Micro Cap)

These indexes spread risk across market caps and stocks and diversifies the out of earnings announcement risk.

On the sector level we can diversify across market segments.

- $IYT (Transports)
- $XBI (Biotech)
- $XLB (Builders)
- $XLE (Energy)
- $XLF (Financial)
- $XLI (Industrials)
- $XLK (Tech)
- $XLP (Consumer Staples)
- $XLRE (Real Estate)
- $XLU (Utilities)
- $XLV (Healthcare)
- $XLY (Consumer Discretionary)

These sector ETFs let you to focus on one sector that may have a different trend than the rest of the sectors or markets. You can rotate to more aggressive or defensive sectors based on the overall stock market phase.

The trend of individual stocks can be determined by many factors, and here are a few.

- The overall stock market trend.
- The sector it's in.
- Whether it's being accumulated or distributed by fund managers.
- Market sentiment for the company's future.
- Change in management.
- Product recalls.
- Accounting scandals.
- Company earnings announcements.
- Company sales trends.

Here is a list of individual stocks that would give a trader focused risk and reward for a single company's results.

- $AAPL
- $AMZN
- $ETSY
- $FIVE
- $GOOGL
- $MA
- $NFLX
- $PYPL
- $SHOP
- $SQ

When you hold these names, your trade is on the company itself. You have little to no diversification, but you receive the full reward if the company exceeds future expectations that are being priced into the stock.

You can also diversify your quantified trading signals based on different strategies. Some buy high in the hopes of selling higher, while others try to create a great risk/reward ratio by buying low, hoping to sell on rebounds or reversals in price action. Different types of trading signals can give you better odds of success across different types of market environments. Here are four types of trading signals.

- Momentum signals are based on buying strength. Momentum traders wait for a strong move in a stock, and then buy and get on-board for a short amount of time. Momentum traders usually trade short time frames like days. These work primarily in bull markets.
- Breakout signals are based on buying all-time highs or 52-week highs, planning to buy high and sell higher. Breakouts are bought trying to catch a parabolic move where a stock

could increase by a large percentage from the entry price over weeks and months. These work primarily in strong bull markets when indexes break to all-time highs.
- Buying oversold dips is based on buying a long-term price support level or an oversold oscillator like the 30 RSI, a price extension far from the 10-day EMA of over 1 or 2 ATRs, or a -80 to -100 $NYMO. This signal attempts to create a great risk/reward ratio based on buying a deep dip of a historical price range. These work best in range-bound markets that become oversold.
- Trend following signals try to go in the direction of the long-term trend by using long term moving averages like the 200-day SMA breaks as buy or sell signals, or all-time highs or lows to enter longs or shorts. These work in trends with higher highs or lower lows.

In addition to diversifying across stock markets, sectors, and assets, you can also trade systems and signals. This allows you to limit your exposure on any one trade, and you can benefit as an edge plays out across multiple market environments.

Don't put all your capital in the same basket at the same time. Instead, spread it around carefully with the right entries and exits based on trends. Trade small, be nimble, be open-minded, and always risk a little and be open to making a lot when the opportunity presents itself. Have a diversified watchlist of the markets that you have signals to trade. Diversify you watchlist across markets, index market caps, sectors, commodities, bonds, and currencies to increase your odds of success.

Diversification and correlation are how you optimize your reward and risk exposure through the correlation of your positions to one another.

9

CASH IS A POSITION

"The desire for constant action irrespective of underlying conditions is responsible for many losses in Wall Street even among the professionals, who feel that they must take home some money every day, as though they were working for regular wages." – Jesse Livermore

A trader who takes a trade based on fear, greed, desperation, or ego instead of a valid entry signal is said to be over trading. Over trading usually happens because a trader wants to be profitable so badly that they ignore their trading plan and allow impulses to influence their decisions. A trader will have an edge over the markets and avoid unnecessary risk if they take trades that meet their entry parameters in a timely manner.

You can greatly decrease your risk by only putting your capital at risk according to a preplanned system, letting it play out over time. When the market doesn't favor your system, it's a better idea to stay in cash rather than forcing trades. Here are some of the dangers of overtrading.

- Over trading in small accounts can rack up large commission costs and reduce profitability. The more you trade the greater the drag your commissions will have on your trading capital. A trade must be worth the round-trip costs of each trade.
- The more you trade the more you pay in slippage. The lower the market volume, the more you lose on each entry and exit based on the distance between the bid and ask.
- The more you trade the more you can be gamed by high frequency traders. If you trade less and trade in a higher time frame, faster traders who operate on shorter time frames (seconds) won't profit on you as much.
- Trading too frequently can lead to bad entries when you should be waiting for good entries. Entries should be based on signals and risk/reward ratios instead of recklessly chasing gains.
- Over trading is bad trading. It's typically the external manifestation of poor self-discipline. It's often the result of not having or not following a trading plan. This is dangerous because you will lose faith in yourself. Only take trades that follow your trading plan after doing the necessary research.

Working longer hours or working harder is how most professions make money, but this isn't true for trading. The best trades come when you're patient and wait for the right entry signal and set up. More trading doesn't necessarily mean more profits, and it's usually the opposite.

Most money is made in trends because big wins usually come from being on the right side of a move for as long as possible. Most of my success has come from being on the right side of a stock or market as it trended for weeks or months. My only input during that time was letting the winner run and checking in at the end of the day to see if anything had changed with my position. Risk is the source of profits, but you should be picky about the risks you take.

These are better places to invest your time and energy than staring at your screen trying to make something happen.Here are a few things that you can do when the market is too dull, too volatile, or you find yourself waiting for an entry signal.

- Backtest new entry and exit parameters.
- Study charts of the best performing stocks in history.
- Study the charts of the worst market crashes.
- Study the charts of the strongest bull markets.
- Look at how your technical indicators perform on charts of indexes and stocks.
- Read trading books.
- Learn how to use all the functions in your charting platform.
- Read great trading blog articles.
- Listen to interviews with great traders.
- Chat with other traders.
- Learn to backtest.
- Take high quality trading eCourses.
- Exercise.
- Go for a walk outdoors.

10

MOVING AVERAGES AS RISK MANAGEMENT TOOLS

"I get very nervous about the retail investor, the average investor, because it's really, really hard. If this was easy, if there was one formula, one way to do it, we'd all be zillionaires. One principle for sure would get out of anything that falls below the 200-day moving average." – Paul Tudor Jones

A moving average is the average price for a trading instrument over a set time frame. They help smooth out the price action and focus on where the current price is trending in relation to an average price, over the trader's time frame.

This is an example of a 10-day moving average.

Chart Courtesy of StockCharts.com

Moving averages are technical tools used on charts for trend identification. They can be used as standalone lines for trend trading, or in conjunction with other technical indicators like MACD, RSI, and price levels of support or resistance. Other moving averages can be combined for crossover signals when a short term moving average crosses over a longer-term moving average of prices.

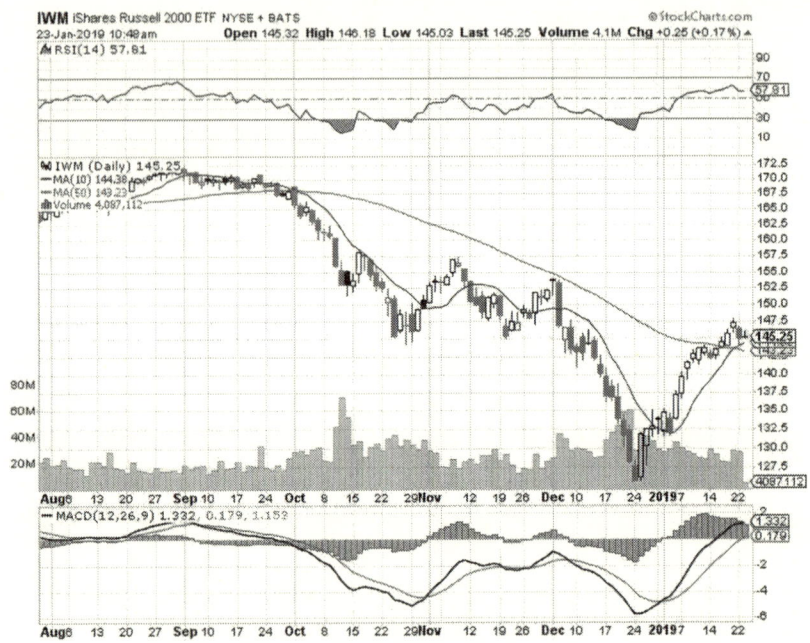

Chart Courtesy of StockCharts.com

A Simple Moving Average (SMA) is an indicator on a chart based on the calculation of the average price of a trading instrument over a set time period. A 5-day simple moving average is the average price over a 5-day period, for example. A simple moving average gives equal weight and importance to all prices in its time period.

An Exponential Moving Average (EMA) gives greater weight to recent prices, to make it more reactive and faster to adjust to price action. An EMA gives traders faster entry and exit signals than a simple moving average.

Moving averages are powerful tools. They are a great place to look when searching for key areas for support and resistance and trend identification. Unlike trend lines that are subjective, moving averages are an unbiased trend indicator based on quantifiable facts. Moving averages can be used on all time frames, intraday, daily, weekly, and monthly.

Moving averages are the simplest of all trend following indicators. In uptrends, price will tend to stay above a key moving average. In downtrends, price will tend to stay below the key moving average. The first possibility of a change in trend is when price crosses through the moving average that it previously had been trending consistently on the other side of. Downtrends start to reverse when prices cross up and through a moving average. Uptrends show signs of reversal when price falls through a moving average and stays below it.

Moving averages are great for entry signals and trend identification, and they're also great risk management tools for financial defense because they allow a trader to create quantified exit signals.

Here are some ways to use moving averages as risk management tools.

- A moving average is a line on a chart that represents the average of prices over a specific time frame, changing as the price changes in the time frame it represents. The curve of the moving average on each time frame is a clue of the path of least resistance of current market price action. A declining moving average can warn a trader on the long side that their market time frame is going into a downtrend. An ascending moving average can warn a short seller that their market is starting to trend back to the upside.
- Moving averages are technical tools that traders use to identify trends on charts. Trading on the right side of the moving average for your time frame reduces the risk of multiple losses in a row, because you'll typically be trading in the direction of the trend. If your trades are held over multiple days in a row, then trading long when price is above the 5-day and 10-day moving averages, and selling short when price is below the 5-day and 10-day moving averages, increases your odds of success on the short-term time frame. Trading against the path of a

moving average increases the risk of a losing streak because the odds are that you are fighting against the current prevailing trend.
- A simple moving average is the average of prices in the time frame. An exponential moving average gives more weight to recent prices and changes faster when reacting to new prices. Exponential moving averages get you in and out of trades faster than simple moving averages, because an EMA will adjust faster to changing prices. You can limit losses in markets with fast moving price action by using EMAs to get you in and out quicker when trades go against you.
- Moving averages can smooth out price action when trading trends. A moving average can tell you when to get into a trade when the breakout price signals a new trend has started and shows you when to get out as price loses support.
- Moving average crossover systems can smooth out volatility for holding positions during a trend. Instead of using one moving average as a signal, you should wait for a faster moving average line to cross over a slower moving average. Filtering volatility and false signals by combining two moving averages gives fewer entry signals and keeps you in a trend for longer periods. This can increase your success during strong trends with a wider initial stop loss, and decrease the risk of over trading by not giving excessive false signals during high volatility environments, when one moving average is not respected by price action.

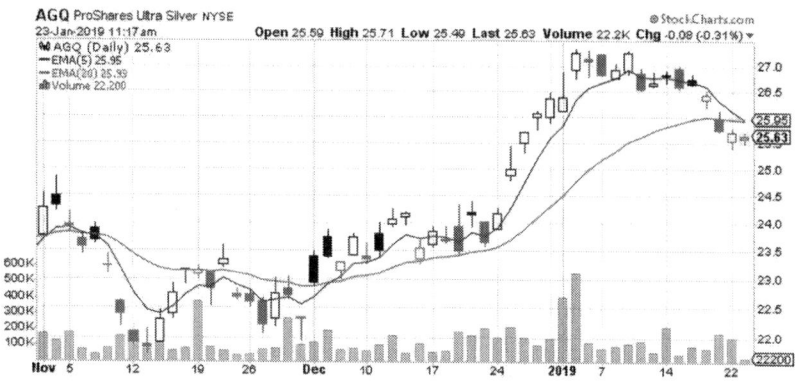

Chart Courtesy of StockCharts.com

- Moving averages are good during trends and aren't useful during sideways markets. If the market you're trading in is going sideways with defined resistance and support, then moving averages aren't the right tools until they converge, and price can get above them all. A confluence of moving averages of different time frames converging at the same time is a clue that your chart isn't trending. Moving averages won't be useful until price can break above all of them and give you the opportunity for a short-term momentum swing to the upside, and the potential start of a new trend. This chart is an example of a confluence of three different moving averages, the 10-day, 50-day, and 100-day to within .41 cents of the same price. This indicates that the chart was range-bound for months. Price closing above the convergence of moving averages would setup a long side trade.

Chart Courtesy of StockCharts.com

- Moving averages can setup good risk/reward ratios in your favor. Moving averages create the potential for big wins and small losses with the ability to let a winner run. You can capture longer-term trends and exit earlier with a small loss during a fast trend reversal when the entry doesn't follow through.
- Moving averages are quantified signals, unlike trend lines that can be discretionary and based on opinions. Moving averages are based on what price action is currently doing and not what someone thinks will happen in the future.
- Moving averages can be backtested for their viability as profitable signals. If a moving average signal worked in the past, it doesn't guarantee it will work in the present, but it increases the odds that it will. Human nature is consistent and trend patterns tend to repeat. You can

build systems that use backtesting data that indicate specific moving averages have worked in the past.
- Moving averages can be used for diversified entry signals. It's less risky to enter a trade when the odds of success are in your favor on your watchlist.
- Moving averages can be used as stop losses to tell you when the odds have shifted against your trade and it's time to take a small loss now to avoid a larger loss in the future.
- A longer-term moving average can be used as a profit target when the risk/reward could shift against you, and it's time to lock in your profits. A long position that has rallied back to the 200-day SMA and stopped, or a short position that has fallen to the 200-day SMA and reversed, are two examples of using a longer-term moving average as a profit target.
- Short term moving averages can be used as trailing stops when you let your winner run until it reverses and closes back under the 10-day EMA.
- Moving average signals can be the foundation of a trend following system when you backtest your own diversified watchlist of stocks or exchange traded funds.

The power of moving averages is that they not only tell you when to get in and make money, but they also tell you when to get out and keep the money you've already made.

11

NEVER RISK YOUR LIFESTYLE

"Speculate with less than 10% of your liquid net worth. Risk less than 1% of your speculative account on a trade. This tends to keep the fluctuations in the trading account small, relative to net worth. This is essential as large fluctuations can engage {emotions} and lead to feeling-justifying drama."
– Ed Seykota

This quote is a rare instance when a Market Wizard quantifies risk management with numbers rather than a metaphor or a universal principle. Let's break down this quote point by point.

First, consider your net worth in cash equivalents. If you're a millionaire based on your stock holdings, retirement funds, bonds, savings, and other cash equivalents, then you have $1,000,000 in these accounts. So according to Mr. Seykota, your active trading account should be $100,000. If your liquid net worth is $100,000, then your active trading account should be $10,000. You can have other types of long-term investments, bonds, real estate, or other types of less aggressive accounts, but your speculative trading capital should only be 10% of your liquid net worth.

You should be able to trade without putting your lifestyle at risk. This removes a lot of the emotions, ego, and stress, because if you blow up your trading account you still have 90% of your net worth intact. The quote is probably targeted at high networth individuals, but you can grow a small account into a big one with consistent returns and compounding capital. Remember that you can also add to your trading account from other sources of income.

Getting rich slowly is usually the best path for people because they learn to appreciate and manage it while they scale their trading system and build on their compounding returns. It's generally not a good idea psychologically to trade with all your money. Trading accounts that are going after aggressive gains through speculative stocks, options, forex, and futures contracts should only be risking capital that they can afford to lose, with the ultimate goal of compounding capital. If the loss of your trading capital is going to affect buying and selling decisions, you are probably trading too large.

Trading accounts are speculative in nature and should be used to grow capital and not a as steady source of income. Trading systems can produce life changing returns during time periods that are conducive to the trading system's signals, but there are times of drawdowns in account equity. In my experience, trading for a living requires being properly capitalized with at least a multiple six figure trading account, depending on your monthly living expenses. Minimizing monthly bills and saving large profit windfalls gives you a chance to work on trading without financial pressure. A spouse that continues to work or multiple streams of income takes a lot of psychological pressure off a professional trader. Trading for a living is a long-term endeavor and requires that you generate profits and compound them over time.

Now let's look at risk from a higher vantage point. The second line of defense in his quote is the 1% total capital at risk per trade. This is what we have already discussed in a previous chapter, but it's worth revisiting here as it is a critical component to successful trading. This is commonly misunderstood by most new traders. The 1% doesn't refer to position size, it refers to the potential of loss.

If you have a $1,000,000 net worth, then you have a $100,000 trading account. If you have a position size of $10,000 in a trade, your trading vehicle would have to drop 10% for you to be down 1% on your trading account. A 10% drop on a position that is a $10,000 position size is $1,000, and $1,000 is 1% of the $100,000 trading account.

The volatility of the trading vehicle and the placement of the stop loss for the position size defines your risk. The quote is explaining that your trading account should be 10% of your net worth and you should risk a 1% loss of your trading capital per trade, which is 0.10% of your net worth risked per trade.

These position sizing parameters and risk management principles will remove the risk of financial ruin, but even more importantly, it will alleviate the risk of emotional ruin. Large losses can cause a trader to lose control, override their trading plan, and self-destruct.

Everyone must start somewhere, so start where you are and begin saving and building your capital. Being undercapitalized is a bad idea for a new trader, because it can be unpleasant when you start actively trading and experience the drag of commissions and bid/ask spreads on a small trading account. The market isn't going anywhere, take your time to build up enough capital for a positive trading experience.

12

MANAGING RISK WITH STOCK OPTIONS

Options are not investments, they are bets on a price in a specific time period. When you buy an option, you pay for the time and volatility dynamics for that bet. An option contract can go to zero and an unhedged, short option play can blow up your account with a large move against you. – Steve Burns

How can an option trader enter a position, risk only $500 of their total trading capital, but control $50,000 worth of stock? The numbers will vary greatly depending on the option pricing, factors of intrinsic value and the Greeks, but the point is that it's possible to control a large dollar value of shares with a small outlay of cash. You're essentially paying for the opportunity to implement leverage using another person's stock. The seller is giving the buyer the opportunity to force the seller to deliver shares if the option goes in the money, and it's called in early or put on the seller at expiration. The buyer of the option is paying for this opportunity. The maximum risk of the option seller is to buy to close the option before expiration at a higher price than they opened, or to deliver or buy shares at the option strike price at expiration.

An option seller who sells a naked option with no hedge theoretically has unlimited risk exposure. Unhedged short options have destroyed many seller accounts over the past 40 years. A way to cap the risk on the short side is to buy a farther out strike option hedge for their short options, or sell options against a stock position that they have, like a covered call or a covered put. This shifts the risk from the short option to your holding moving against you.

Option sellers can experience long-term winning streaks and may start to feel invincible. They may start to think, why in the world would I *not* trade options? Then an event like Black Monday 1987, or the financial panic in the fall of 2008 happen, and selling naked put options leads to total ruin. I highly recommend selling options with a hedge in place, so your risk is capped to the strike price of your farther out of the money hedge, and your worst-case scenario is a manageable loss rather than an empty account.

There is an option play called a *credit spread* that lets you sell option premium and buy an option farther out of the money, as a hedge for your short option. For example, if a stock is trading at $97, you could sell an out-of-the-money $100 strike call option at $3 and then go out farther in strike price on the same time frame, buying a $105 strike call option for $1. This drops your profit potential from $300 to $200 in the option play, but it caps your loss to $300 if the stock moves all the way to $105 instead of a potential unlimited loss.

For this bearish credit spread to be profitable, price must close below $102 at expiration, or the short side of the option play bought back for a profit before expiration. If the stock closes below $100 on the day of expiration, then the option expires worthless and the trade will net you $200 in profits. Over $102, and the trade is a loser and could cost you up to $300 if the stock runs all the way to $105. Your long option hedge then kicks in and limits your loss to $300. If the stock price plunges lower and drops the short option value enough, it could be worth closing early to lock in profits.

An important lesson for new traders is that an option can be traded at any time before expiration. You don't have to wait to trade an option until expiration to be profitable. It can be hard to exit the long option hedge side of your trade if your short side is profitable, because the liquidity will dry up on options so far out of the money. The long hedge will often be a full loss if your short side is profitable.

One concern about selling stocks short is that there's theoretically unlimited risk because a stock price has no ceiling. If you buy a stock at $5, it can go to zero and you lose your initial $5 per share. However, if you short a $5 stock, it can go to $100 and you will lose $95 a share. This is an extreme example, and traders should exit long before this happens. Penny stocks and biotech stocks can be dangerous on the short side, if you can find shares to borrow and sell short. Selling short during an uptrend and letting a losing short position run hoping it will reverse can lead to large losses.

Buying put options in place of short selling solves a couple of problems for stock traders that want to play the short side. You don't have to worry about finding shares to borrow for a short sell, you only need to make sure the put options are liquid for your time frame, and that your loss is limited to the put option contract. If a stock gaps up against your put option, then your risk is already defined and capped at the price of your contract. If your put option contract is less than 1% of your total trading capital, then the damage and drawdown will be minimal to your trading career.

Your long-put options can also go up in value if the volatility of the underlying stock increases as the Vega value will increase. However, Vega cuts both ways and your long-put options can drop in value quickly during market rallies, as the VIX drops and the Vega value decays quickly with fear and uncertainty decreasing. A rising VIX and an expanding price range will drive up put option values, making them more expensive to buy later in a downtrend. They will be scooped up as hedges for insurance on longer term positions by investors and money managers. I think that put options is the safest way to sell stocks short to cap your risk during unexpected rallies.

The power of owning options is in the opportunity to provide leverage to capital and to cap the risk exposure. For a relatively small amount of capital, an option trader can control 100 shares of stock. By owning high Delta in-the-money options, you can capture a large percentage of a price move with a limited risk exposure, regardless of the size or speed of a move. In the long run, large losses are avoided by having a long option hedge for short option plays. This will pay for itself during unexpected market moves.

This is the power of asymmetric trading, unlimited upside with a limited downside. A key to managing risk in options is to avoid risking too much capital on any one trade. Instead, you can use option contracts to control the same shares of stocks that you would if you properly position sized a stock trade at 10% of your trading capital. The biggest mistake that new option traders make is to trade too large and their first loss or string of losses is the end of their trading career.

Many people fear options because they can be all or nothing trades. The key to managing that aspect of option trading is to trade with amounts that can be meaningful if you win, but not devastating if you lose. It's the big winning trades and winning streaks that can pay for many small losses. The option seller has the risk in the underlying stock of the option, but the buyer has the upside and the risk of the contract price. Options don't need stops because they have built in stops by their very nature. The important part is the position sizing on entry.

Never lose more than 1% of your total trading capital on one option trade. If you have a $30,000 option trading account, then you can only buy options worth $300 or less per trade. This caps your worst-case scenario loss at 1%, and it would take 10 losing trades in a row for a 10% drawdown in total trading capital. It may be possible to buy a $600 option with a 50% stop loss, but that is an arbitrary level to exit. The best stop loss for options should be based on key price levels on stock charts that invalidated your original entry, just like a stock losing its price support when you are long with a call option position. Trading longer out options can provide more leeway with stops because their Deltas are lower, and you are trading primarily with slow moving Theta time decay.

Options are not risky trading vehicles in themselves; it's the asymmetric nature of your trades and the risk exposure you create or hedge that determines whether or not they are risky.

This is just a brief look at Options. If you would like to learn more about options, you can check out our book on Amazon and eCourse at NewTraderU.com devoted entirely to options trading.

13

CAUSES OF TRADING LOSSES

"Trade small because that's when you are as bad as you are ever going to be. Learn from your mistakes." – Richard Dennis

1. A small win
2. A big win
3. A small loss
4. Break even

All of your trades should end in one of these four ways. You should never experience a big loss. Removing a large loss as one of the outcomes in your system will increase your odds of success. Unprofitability is almost guaranteed if you endure large losses, and can even lead to ruin during losing streaks. If you can limit large losses you have a better chance of being a successful trader for years to come.

A small win increases your account size and helps to counteract small losses. A small win is good but not the ideal outcome. Small wins mean you must have a large winning percentage to achieve profitability. The old Wall Street adage, "You can't go broke taking a profit," isn't accurate. You can take your account to zero if you consistently have large losses and small wins. Also, if you have small wins and small losses with a 50% win-rate, commissions and slippage can result in unprofitability.

Profitability comes from large wins and this is the path of least resistance for most traders, regardless if it's buy and hold investing playing long-term stock trends, or trend following catching a 6-week trend in a commodity. The big wins pay for a lot of small losses. If you want to make money in the markets, then learning how to structure your trading to capture the most profit is a good place to start.

A small loss is the cost of doing business. When the trade doesn't work out and price moves against you and triggers your exit signal, it's time to take the loss while it's small. All traders experience small losses and no trading system is 100% accurate. A good trader will cut the loss, while a less experienced trader will hold and hope. When a trader gets stuck on the wrong side of a trend and stays there, the small loss can evolve into a devastating one.

A break-even trade is rare, but it can happen if a market goes nowhere and you exit your trade on a time stop, or see a better opportunity for capital allocation somewhere else.

Large losses generally come from a combination of greed and ego. When you add some leverage, it can be very expensive to be wrong about a trade. Large losses must be managed through proper position sizing and the right stop loss placement based on the asset's historical volatility. Stop losses must be honored when they're triggered. Here are the top reasons for large losses.

- A trader is too stubborn to exit when proven wrong: They refuse to take a loss and think it isn't real until they exit the trade. Not exiting with a small loss puts you on the wrong side of a trend and ties up your trading capital that could be used to make money somewhere else.

- Too much ego to take a loss: When a trader is on the wrong side of the market trend but thinks that if they hold a losing position they can be proven right on a reversal. While they're waiting to be proven right, their losses get larger. In this case, they care more about being right than they do about losing money.
- Too much hope for a reversal: They think the market can't keep moving against them and must reverse at current price levels. They think that the market must reverse around a key support or resistance price level, but bull markets have no long-term resistance and bear markets have no long-term support levels. A breakout of a price range changes the dynamics of price action.
- Trading too big a position size: The bigger you trade, the greater your potential for loss and the more likely it is that you'll panic and not follow your trading plan. If you trade a large position size, even a small move against you can result in a large loss. Keeping losses small starts with proper position sizing.
- Buying in a downtrend: Bulls in bear markets lose money as markets make lower highs and lower lows. All stocks and sectors eventually go down in bear markets. A company's potential doesn't matter when equities as an asset class are being distributed by money managers raising cash for investor's redemptions. Stocks are only good if they are going up.
- Selling short in an uptrend: Bears in bull markets lose money as the market makes higher highs and higher lows. Being stubbornly bearish and short when a market has signaled an uptrend can result in large losses when a short position moves farther against you in an uptrend, and you don't buy to cover your position early in the rally.
- No trading plan: When you don't have a plan for your

trades you plan to fail. If you don't have position sizing parameters, stop loss guidelines, and risk management rules embedded in your system, you are setting yourself up for heartache. If you don't know how you'll avoid large losses, you probably won't.
- No trading system: If you don't have a quantified and backtested price action trading system, then you're just trading randomly. You'll experience large losses due to the random nature of entries, exits, position sizing, and stop losses. If you haven't defined what your risk/reward ratio is in your trading system, then your risk may be larger than you suspect.
- Bad position sizing parameters: Big losses will occur when position sizing is not based on historical volatility, current volatility, and worst-case scenarios. If your position sizing is based on the belief that nothing bad will happen or best-case scenarios, you are probably in danger.
- No discipline: Not doing the work to create a systematic trading process or not being disciplined enough to follow a predetermined method will consistently cause you problems. You must do your homework before you start trading by reading, researching, developing a tested system, and setting up risk management guidelines. In the end, you must have the discipline to execute when the market is open, what you planned to do when the market was closed.

A lot of profitable trading will come down to how disciplined you are with position sizing and stop losses, and how quickly you admit you're wrong in a trade that is going against you. If none of your trades end with a large loss, you have a significant edge in the markets.

14

THE BIGGEST TRADING LOSSES IN HISTORY

"Fish see the bait, but not the hook; men see the profit, but not the peril." – Chinese proverb

If you ever feel down about your trading losses or drawdown from your equity peak, this chapter may put your own losses into perspective. The losses in this chapter show how crucial it is to have a price level that will indicate that you were wrong so you can stop a loss from becoming devastating for your account and your psyche.

There's never a good reason to take a large loss to your trading capital. Growing capital comes second to position sizing, stop losses, and managing the risk of ruin. If you don't blow up your account, you may be around long enough to benefit from gains in the market that fits your own trading method. As you will see from the following examples of the largest trading losses in history, professionals are not immune from the dangers of risk. The greater the pursuit of big gains and fast profit, the larger the risk and chance of failure. Heed the lessons of these stories and give yourself an edge.

- German billionaire Adolf Merckle, one of the 100 richest people in the world, killed himself by jumping in front of a train. He was said to be emotionally broken over a bad bet on Volkswagen in 2008. Rival Porsche silently cornered the market on Volkswagen shares, and when they revealed the extent of their stake, the price of Volkswagen stock shot up to levels that made it briefly the world's most valuable corporation. Many hedge funds who had bet against Volkswagen, like Merckle, lost huge amounts of money, while Porsche made billions in profit.
- His personal wealth was estimated at more than $9 billion, and he reportedly lost a billion on the Volkswagen stock. The loss led to margin calls from other creditors and threatened to unravel his entire business empire. Full Article
- Nelson Bunker Hunt and William Herbert Hunt, the sons of Texas oil billionaire Haroldson Lafayette Hunt, Jr., tried for some time to corner the market in silver. The Hunt brothers invested heavily in futures contracts with several brokers, including the brokerage firm Bache Halsey Stuart Shields, later Prudential-Bache Securities and Prudential Securities. When the price of silver dropped below their minimum margin requirement, they were issued a margin call for $100 million. The Hunts were unable to meet the margin call, and, with the brothers facing a potential $1.7 billion loss, the ensuing panic was felt in the financial markets. Many government officials feared that if the Hunts were unable to pay their debts, some Wall Street brokerage firms and banks could collapse. In the end, a consortium of US banks provided a $1.1 billion line of credit to the brothers, allowing them to pay Bache. The US Securities and Exchange Commission (SEC) later launched an investigation into the Hunt brothers, who failed to

disclose that they held a 6.5% stake in Bache. Full Article
- Under the leadership of CEO Heinz Schimmelbusch, German metals and engineering giant Metallgellschaft was on the brink of bankruptcy after losing $1.3 billion on speculative trades. The firm bet on an increase in oil prices in oil futures markets, but oil prices dropped instead. Full Article
- Robert Citron lost $1.7 billion for Orange County, California forcing it into Chapter 9 bankruptcy. In 1994, Citron was Treasurer-Tax Collector for Orange County, California. As treasurer, Citron used a series of highly leveraged deals that included repurchase agreements and floating rate notes. Full Article
- A lot of success in the financial markets comes from navigating short term volatility. When fund managers fail to identify informational asymmetries, bad things happen. This played out in the downfall of the LTCM fund, which was set in motion prior to the 1997 East Asian financial crisis. In May and June of 1998, returns from the fund were -6.42% and -10.14% respectively, reducing LTCM's capital by $461 million. This was further exasperated by the exit of Salomon Brothers from the arbitrage business in July 1998. The losses were accentuated when the Russian government defaulted on their government bonds, causing a financial crisis in August and September of 1998. Panicked investors sold Japanese and European bonds to buy US treasury bonds, and the profits that were supposed to occur as the value of these bonds converged became large losses when the value of the bonds diverged. By the end of August, LTCM had lost $1.85 billion in capital. As a result, LTCM had to liquidate several of its positions at a highly

unfavorable moment and suffer further losses. After many forced liquidations, LTCM suffered substantial losses. The company, which was providing annual returns of almost 40% up to this point, experienced a flight-to-liquidity. In the first three weeks of September, LTCM's equity tumbled from $2.3 billion at the start of the month to just $400 million by September 25. With liabilities still over $100 billion, this translated to an effective leverage ratio of more than 250-to-1. Full Article

- In September of 2011, UBS revealed an unexpected $2.3 billion loss believed to be caused by a lone rogue trader in the bank's London office. Kweku Adoboli, 31, who worked on UBS's Delta One desk, was identified as the alleged rogue trader. This unfortunate event led to the resignation of UBS's CEO. Full Article
- In 2008, a Brazilian pulp maker lost $2.5 billion on currency bets. At the time, Aracruz was the world's biggest producer of bleached eucalyptus-pulp. In 2008, the firm lost a large amount on Forex trades when it bet that the Brazilian real would appreciate in an effort to hedge against a weaker dollar. The Brazilian real ended up tanking. Full Article
- In 1996, Sumitomo's chief trader, Yasuo Hamakana, nicknamed Mr. Five Percent and Mr. Copper, attempted to corner the copper market on the London Metal Exchange with his aggressive style and lost $2.6 billion. He went to prison. Full Article
- Société Générale Bank officials claim that throughout 2007, Jerome Kerviel was trading profitably in anticipation of falling market prices. He was subsequently accused of exceeding his authority to engage in unauthorized trades which totaled as much as

€49.9 billion, a figure far higher than the bank's total market capitalization. Bank officials claim that Kerviel tried to conceal the activity by intentionally creating losing trades to offset his early gains. According to the BBC, Kerviel generated €1.4 billion in hidden profits by the end of 2007, until his employers uncovered the unauthorized activity and closed out the positions at the beginning of 2008. This came at a time when the market was experiencing a large drop in equity indices, and losses were estimated at €4.9 billion. Full Article

- In April 2005, Brian Hunter was reportedly offered a $1 million bonus to leave Amaranth Advisors and join SAC Capital Partners. Nicholas Maounis, founder of Amaranth Advisors, refused to let Hunter go. Maounis named Hunter co-head of the firm's energy desk and gave him control of his own trades. In 2006, his analysis detailed how 2006-2007 winter gas prices would rise. Hunter went long on the winter delivery contracts, simultaneously shorting the near (summer/fall) contracts. When the market took a sharp turn against him, the fund was hard pressed for margin money to maintain the positions. Once the margin requirements crossed 3 billion USD in September 2006, the fund offloaded some of the positions, selling them to JP Morgan and Citadel for 2.5 billion USD. In the end, the fund took a $6.6-billion loss and had to be dissolved. Full Article
- Bruno Michel Iksil, nicknamed the London Whale (for his risky trades) and Voldemort (for his supposed power over Wall Street) is a trader who worked for the London office of JPMorgan Chase who is responsible for losses up to $9 billion. He reportedly began working for JPMorgan in 2005 and lives in Paris. Full Article
- Hubler, a former mortgage trader at Morgan Stanley featured in Michael Lewis' "The Big Short," lost the bank

$9 billion on bets in the subprime housing market in 2007. Full Article

The risk of ruin is ever present for traders and money managers that fail to respect the risk of ruin and refuse to that make contingency plans if they're wrong.

AFTERWORD

"That cotton trade was almost the deal breaker for me. It was at that point that I said, "Mr. Stupid, why risk everything on one trade?" Why not make your life a pursuit of happiness rather than pain?" – Paul Tudor Jones

If you start with how much you are risking and quantify the cost of being wrong, then you can work on the reward of being right. Every risk you take with your hard-earned money must be worth the time, stress, and potential returns. If you're making money, let your winners run for as long as you can in your time frame. If you're losing money on a trade, ask yourself why you're still in it.

The best trades usually reward you by showing that the trade will be a winner from the start. The worst trades usually go against you immediately, and this is especially true for traders on shorter time frames. The only reason to trade is in the pursuit of profits. If you're not making money in a system over a long period of time, what's the point?

Trading is about one-third psychology, one-third system, and one-third risk management. If you don't have all three in place, then none of it works. I hope this book helps you with the risk management piece of the trading puzzle.

ABOUT THE AUTHORS

Steve Burns started investing in 1993 and trading his own accounts in 1995. It was love at first trade. A natural teacher with a unique ability to cut through the bull and make complex ideas simple, Steve wrote New Trader Rich Trader and started New Trader U in 2011.

When Holly met Steve in 2014, she knew they could take his trading knowledge to the next level. Acting as CTO and co-author, Holly has helped Steve publish 13 best-selling books and six popular eCourses for NewTraderUniversity.com.

READY TO TAKE YOUR TRADING TO THE NEXT LEVEL?

Join thousands of other traders at NewTraderUniversity.com and learn from Steve and benefit from more than 25 years of trading success!

Did you enjoy this eBook?

Please consider writing a review.

Listen to many of our titles on Audio!

Read more bestselling titles:

New Trader Rich Trader (Revised and Updated)

New Trader Rich Trader 2 (Revised and Updated)

The Ultimate Price Action Trading Guide

Moving Averages 101

So You Want to be a Trader

New Trader 101

Moving Averages 101

Buy Signals and Sell Signals

Trading Habits

Investing Habits

Calm Trader